Prayer As Dance

Choreography of Grace

Prayer As Dance invites you to deepen your relationship with God through the dialogue of prayer. This book does not present a formula for prayer, but rather a strategy for discovering the astonishing, transforming experience of talking with God.

Each chapter is comprised of a brief introduction, Scripture passages, questions, and a Personal Reflection and Personal Response section. In addition; there are poems, quotations, and essays which will spark awareness of God's grace. Your invitation to worship was sent before you were born. It is found in Psalm 150: 3-4.

I have personally known God's indelible grace throughout this journey of life. Just shy of my first birthday, doctors told my mother I would not survive a mysterious illness.

When it became evident I would live, the probability I would not be able to walk was the next dire prediction on the horizon.

Physicians were relying on their knowledge of the science of Pediatric medicine. They were

Continued on inside back cover...

2018

*Prayer is the language
of love.*

Patti Gell

Prayer As Dance

Patti A. Gell

The purpose of Prayer As Dance is to spark a renewed awareness of the dynamic relationship God invites us to experience with Him. Prayer was designed by God as dialogue. It is one of the central means God uses to reveal Himself to us.

Weaving together quiet reflections on prayer with a thoughtful study of God's Word , Prayer As Dance is a guide to cultivating a vibrant and intimate relationship with the Living God.

Each chapter is designed to encourage readers to create space for the beauty of God's grace to shimmer through their life. In the process, we discover the essence of who we are is exactly the person God created us to become.

Third Printing

NU Publishing • Scottsdale, AZ
ISBN: 978-0-615-40051-8

Dedication

To my mother; Mae Ferguson Pendleton,
whose winsome smile, ceaseless prayers and
enduring faith, continue to inspire those who knew
her. I know she is dancing with her Savior today.
May this book pay tribute to a life lived with honor.

PRAYER DANCE

Pleasure of His Company

Reflection / Confession

Abiding in Him

Yielding to His choreography

Embrace His goodness

Rest in His embrace

Desiring God

Accept His Invitation

Notice His presence

Connect with others

Express His love through my life

Contents

Let them praise His name with dancing,
for the Lord takes delight in His people.

Psalm 149:3-4

Acknowledgements

Gratitude is grace in Sunday clothes.

Gratitude for this book is extended as praise to my Savior, Jesus Christ. How is it He transformed a Bible Study about prayer and grace and faith into this book - which serves as a reminder that He invites us to dance with Him everyday?

My publisher encouraged and cajoled me throughout this process. He believed in the message of this book when my vision was blurred by discouragement. Thank you, Bill.

To the great teachers and writers who always inspire me; Phillip Keller, Henri Nouwen, Cynthia Heald, David Foster, Corrie Ten Boom, and Ben Patterson.

I am eternally grateful to my husband and best friend, Bob. Thank you for your support and confidence.

To the precious women and men who prayed for me during this process, I can only say, "You are amazing".

Finally, with overwhelming gratitude, I thank the women of the Prayer As Dance – Invitation To Intimacy pilot class. Their encouragement and commission to write this book has been my inspiration. Grace and love to you: Amy, Betty, Elsie, Jodi, Joanne, Lyndsey, May, Susie, and Nancy.

Introduction

Dancing With The Stars has become one of the most popular programs on TV. Each week millions of people are captivated by this artistic expression of dance.

It is not surprising we find pleasure in the exquisite beauty of a skillfully choreographed dance. God designed us with a capacity for joyful expression. According to Scripture, the expression of praise takes many forms, including dance. Haven't you experienced moments of joy and exhilaration that flow from being aware of the essence of the Spirit of God? There is within us a restlessness to cultivate an intimate relationship with Christ.

This book invites the reader to become spiritually transparent, and nurture relationships which reflect an authentic quality. The format facilitates the awareness that God invites us to praise Him with "dancing, and harp and lyre". (Psalms 150:4)

To this end, there are eleven Rehearsals. We title the chapters, Rehearsals, because rehearsals are not performance. Rehearsals provide time to stand quietly until we hear the notes as they were composed for us. Each tenuous step of faith is followed by another and another and another. Through practice we gain confidence to share the dance with protégés we meet along the way.

Each Rehearsal is comprised of a brief introduction to the topic, scripture passages and questions to answer. At the end of each Rehearsal, there is a Personal Reflection and Personal Response section. These exercises will assist the reader in enlarging and personalizing the principles in the Rehearsal.

In addition to Rehearsals, there are poems, quotations and essays to spark attentiveness to the manifestation of God's transforming grace.

The precepts shared in this book are not presented as definitive truth, but rather discreetly, inviting you to discover your own rhythm. As with any complex dance routine, it is only through practice, that prayer becomes uniquely integrated into the routine of our days.

The Choreographer of the dance invites us to worship Him through the intimate sacrament of prayer. The dictionary defines choreography as dance writing. The art of making structures in which movement occurs. It is also defined as a sequence of messages, focusing on the exchange of information. Isn't that a beautiful definition of prayer? Prayer is an exchange of messages between God and His people. It is intended to be dialogue, not monologue. Through the relationship of prayer, we discover the essence of the person God created us to become.

Your invitation was sent before you were born. It is found in Psalm 150:4. See you at Rehearsal...

I Want To Dance With You

Me? Was He really asking me to dance?
I looked into His eyes. I longed to say yes. He asked again, "May I have this dance?" With a winsome smile, He took me by the hand. "Oh Yes! I want to dance with You", I replied.

As the music began, I was able to speak of my heart's desire: "You understand my every longing, I know that You do. For too long this dance has been solo. As I step into Your embrace, teach me the choreography of loving You. I want to bask in Your love and return that love through the symphony of my life. Create in me the desire to move through my world In step with You, dancing in tune with the music that is mine.

Teach me the dance of suffering. As we glide to a mournful ballet, choreograph my steps. Take me by the hand and "turn my mourning into dancing". Teach me Your secret steps, O Dancer, breathe into my being the breath of energy and light as we celebrate the rhythm of creation.

Pause with me and illustrate the galaxies above. Introduce me to The Keeper of the stars. Dance with me in the silence….. Hold me in the storm. And when the orchestra plays the final note, I will take your hand and say; "I want to dance with You. I want to dance with You."

Suggestions For Solo Rehearsal
Put on Your Dancing Shoes....

Begin with prayer. Pause to acknowledge you are approaching this rehearsal anticipating intimate moments with the Savior.

Be willing to try on new shoes. Invite the Spirit to expand the knowledge you have acquired. Read the introduction and the Personal Reflection for the Rehearsal before you begin your study. This will assist you in being mindful of the purpose of the lesson.

Read the Scripture references which accompany each question. Questions are based on NIV. Use your favorite translation.

Answer a few questions each day. Answers can be as short or lengthy as you choose. Sometimes one word is enough. Try to complete one Rehearsal each week. You may enjoy using a journal or a notebook to record your answers and reflections.

End your Rehearsal as you began, with prayer. Small efforts when given with integrity have enormous impact. Ask for wisdom to apply concepts from each Rehearsal while becoming more attentive to God's presence each day.

Suggestions For Small Group Study
Put on Your Dancing Shoes....

Confidentiality is essential. What is shared in the group stays in the group.

Make a commitment to attend Rehearsal each week. You are important to the success of the class. Life happens. It is understood you may not be at each Rehearsal. When you are absent, please know your unique contributions will be missed. Come to Rehearsal prepared to participate in the discussion. This is not a lecture format. Your leader will facilitate the dialogue but each member of the group is significant to the success of the class.

Be sensitive to other class participants. Try to limit your responses to the Rehearsal topic being discussed. This will allow time for everyone to participate. Listen attentively. Respect and tolerance are the currency of friendship. Expect that you will build intimacy with the Savior not only from the Scripture passage, but also as you consider insights shared by others. God created us wonderfully complex and unique individuals. The choreography for my life will be somewhat different from yours. Trust the Holy Spirit to bring synergy as we glean knowledge from one another. Ask for grace to be attentive to incorporate the precepts of each Rehearsal into practical application during the week. Pray for one another.

It is not our prayer that moves Jesus.
It is Jesus who moves us to pray.
He knocks, making known His desire to come in.

O. Hallesby

The Pleasure of His Company

Rehearsal One

Jesus is a gentleman. He never forces His way into our lives. Revelation 3:20 tells us He stands at the door and knocks. Listen! Is He waiting at your door now? Perhaps He is asking, "Will you dance with me?"

> Have you had someone knock at your door when you were not expecting guests? How did you respond?

> Can you think of any benefits you might experience if you invite someone into your home even though you were not expecting them?

> Picture Jesus standing at your door. What are some reasons that you might not want to invite Him in?

Jesus frequently invited persons into closer relationship by asking a question or making a statement which challenged the person to think about who He is and to examine their perception of Him.

Read John 20:10-18
Mary is in the depth of grief. Her beloved friend is dead. She does not recognize Jesus is the one speaking to her. Jesus asked, "Who is it you are looking for?"

What did Jesus say that caused Mary to recognize Him?

Do you think it was hearing her name spoken, or Jesus' tone of voice that transformed the moment for Mary?

How would you respond if Jesus asked, "Who are you looking for?" How might your answer enrich the relationship you have with Him?

Read Matthew 16:13-20. How would you respond to Jesus question, "Who do you say I am?"

Who Is Doing The Dishes?
Read Luke 10:38 – 41

In this narrative, Jesus invites us to become unseen guests in the home of two sisters, Mary and Martha. This passage recounts the details of His visit to their home in Bethany. Both women loved Jesus dearly, yet each one demonstrated her love in a very different manner.

From verse 40, list at least two methods Martha uses to express her concern for Jesus comfort and her devotion to Him.

How did Mary demonstrate her delight at having Jesus in her home?

In verse 42, Jesus tells Martha only one thing is needed. Based on His response, what do you think He is referring to?

Through His conversation with Martha, Jesus seems to be reminding us of the need to set priorities. What obstacles do you encounter that prevent you from "sitting at the feet of Jesus?"

Personal Reflection
Prayer is a language of love. God says, "You are concerned about many things, but only one thing is needed". As we savor the pleasure of His company, we become attuned to the gentle nudge of God's spirit guiding us. His choreography becomes the expressive language of our life.

Personal Response
Spend a few minutes reflecting on the question: "Who is it you are looking for?" (John 20:15) You may wish to write in your journal, sing a song, write a poem, take a nature walk, or spend a few moments in prayer as you reflect on this lesson.

Prayer does not change God
but it changes the person who prays

Soren Kierkegaard

Reflection / Confession

Rehearsal Two

Isaiah 53

Isaiah 53:1-12 (The Message)
Who believes what we've heard and seen?
Who would have thought God's saving power would look like this?

The servant grew up before God – a scrawny seedling, a scrubby plant in a parched field. There was nothing attractive about him, nothing to cause us to take a second look. He was looked down and passed over, a man who suffered, who knew pain firsthand. One look at him and people turned away. We looked down on him, thought he was scum. But the fact is, it was our pains he carried – our disfigurements, all the things wrong with us.

We thought he brought it on himself, that God was punishing him for his own failures. But it was our sins that did that to him, that ripped and tore and crushed him – our sins! He took the punishment, and that made us whole.

Through his bruises we get healed. We're all like sheep who've wandered off and gotten lost. We've done our own thing, gone our own way. And God piled all our sins, everything we've done wrong on him, on him. He was beaten, he was tortured, but he didn't say a word. Like a lamb taken to be slaughtered and like a sheep being sheared, he took it all in silence.

Justice miscarried, and he was led off and did anyone really know what was happening? He died without a thought for his own welfare, beaten bloody for the sins of my people. They buried him with the wicked, threw him in a grave with a rich man, even though he'd never hurt a soul or said one word that wasn't true. Still, it's what God had in mind all along, to crush him with pain.

The pain was that he give himself as an offering for sin so that he'd see life come from it – life, life, and more life.

And God's plan will deeply prosper through him.

Rehearsal Two

When you hear the word confession, what comes to mind? Confession has two distinct applications, both of which are commanded in scripture. The apostle Paul tells us in Romans 10:9, "If you confess with your mouth, "Jesus is Lord," and believe in your heart, that God raised Him from the dead, you will be saved." This is known as the creedal statement of confession.

The other application we learn from scripture is the instruction to confess our sin. Confession is admitting or acknowledging sin. When the light of God's holiness shines upon us, we begin to see our lives from His perspective. Jesus is holy and without sin. I John 1: 9 tell us when we confess our sin; Jesus is faithful to forgive us. Corrie Ten Boom says God not only forgives our sins, he throws them in the deepest ocean and posts "No Fishing" signs. (Psalm 103:10-12)

Read John 20:24-29

> How did Thomas respond when he recognized Jesus?

Jesus respected Thomas' doubts about His resurrection. He knew Thomas was not just being stubborn, but rather seeking answers to his questions. Often, persons who are seeking truth have doubts. God is not afraid of our questions. Doubt can be a tool to deepen our faith when we earnestly seek God through scripture, prayer and trusted Christian friends. God provided a Book with 66 chapters filled with information. This Bible, God's love letter to us, contains the answers to our questions so we, along with Thomas, can confess, "My Lord and my God".

Read II Timothy 2:19

> What is required of those who confess, "Jesus is Lord"?

The previous question provides the perfect segue to examine the other side of the coin of confession. Confession, in this application, is to acknowledge or confess our sin. In the Greek New Testament, the word confess, means to speak the same thing that God speaks. We are to be in agreement with Him. The essence of intimacy with Christ is to pray in agreement with God and live in transparency with Him.

Read Amos 3:3 & 7

> What does this passage say about living in agreement with God?

Read II Chronicles 7:14

> List the four measures Solomon outlines in

this verse which demonstrate genuine confession.

_____

_____

_____

_____

What three things does God promise He will do in response to our confession?

_____

_____

_____

Read Psalm 32:3-7
(David pours out the anguish of unconfessed sin in this Psalm.)

Did David suffer physical symptoms as a result of his alienation from God?

How were they manifest?

What was the first step in his healing?

What was God's response?

35

Read I John 1:8-10

How do we experience God's forgiveness?

Read Ephesians 2:8-9

What must we do to earn God's grace?

Personal Reflection

According to Proverbs 6:17, one of the seven things God hates is lying. Discreetly known as the dance of deception, lying is one of the most harmful habits or attitudes that contributes to the destruction of relationships. How can one be intimate with a person whom one does not trust? When God gave the Ten Commandments, (they are not suggestions) he did not stay awake all night devising an obstacle course of rules and regulations. No. Every command has love written across it. When we miss the mark He has set for us, confession is the key to restored intimacy with God.

David knew the agony of broken fellowship and the joy of reconciliation. David danced before the Lord in praise.

Are you aware the Lord rejoices over you?

"The Lord your God is with you. He is mighty to save. He will take great delight in you, He will quiet you with His love, He will rejoice over you with singing." (Zephaniah 3:17)

Personal Response

When we examine the Bible, God's Love Letter carefully, it is evident the desire of God's heart is not only that we know Him, but also that we be known by Him. Confession is the avenue God uses to restore the brokenness in our lives. David made mistakes, but he was willing to be transparent before God, accept His forgiveness and move on. Unconfessed sin hinders intimacy.

Write your definition of confession as an expression of love to God.

God speaks in the silence of the heart.
Listening is the beginning of prayer.

Mother Teresa

Abiding In Him

Rehearsal Three

In this Rehearsal, we will consider how abiding in Christ empowers us to radiate God's gracious spirit into our world. We will affirm God is our shelter and our strength.

The dictionary definition of abide is to dwell or reside. There are countless illustrations in Scripture of abiding in Christ. One of the most referenced passages is John 15. In this example, Jesus uses the visual image of the vine and branches to teach His disciples the importance of staying connected to Him.

We have all experienced days when life is so stressful we hurry home, shut the door, and close the world out. It matters not if we are in five o'clock traffic, struggling with a two year old, or deciding which bills to pay this month, the shelter of His everlasting arms becomes reality when we step into the security of God's love.

David acknowledges in Psalm 59, that God's constant love is a place of safety in a frightening world. The invitation Christ extends to intimacy, includes the assurance that He is trustworthy.

But I will sing of your strength, in the morning I sing of your love; for You are my fortress, my refuge in time of trouble.   Psalm 59:16

Read Psalm 91:1-6

Who does the author of this Psalm trust?

How does he indicate we can experience this protection and level of trust?

Who or what has broken "trust" in your life? Do you think it impacts you today?

How and in what ways?

In practical terms, how can we "dwell in the shelter of the most High"?

Which character quality of God does the Psalmist say is our shield?

Read Psalm 91:9-16

In this Psalm, notice God does not promise we will not face danger or difficulty.
He does promise to be with us through the difficulty.

What reason does the Lord give for His protection?

When will He answer our cry for help?

Which verse or verses were especially meaningful to you from Psalm 91? Why?

Read John 15:4

> Jesus makes a promise in this verse. What is it? What does He require of us?

> What motivational statement does Jesus make to inspire us to remain in Him?

We began by reading from Psalm 91, that God is our dwelling place. From these closing passages, we learn that God lives in believers. Not only do we live in Him, He lives in us.

Read Leviticus 26:11-12

> God invites us to make our dwelling with Him. In this passage, where does He promise to reside?

Read Ephesians 2:22

> How does the reality of Christ living in us, impact our confidence during difficult times?

Personal Reflection

The performance of beautiful dance transpires when there is synchronization between partners. A ballroom dancer recently told me he leads from the shoulders. His partner must trust that he will guide her through the execution of intricate steps. It is essential they be engaged; mind, body and spirit to conclude the dance.

Jesus invites us to unreservedly abide in Him. During this Rehearsal, have you affirmed you can trust Him in the storms of life? Do you have confidence in the choreography He has written for you?

Personal Response:

Memorize the verse(s) you found meaningful from Psalm 91. Are there trust issues that affect your personal relationships and impact your spiritual transparency?

Meditate on the essay **I Want To Dance With You** (page 17).

When we confide our doubts and disappointments, we create space for healing to begin.

Prayer is exhaling the spirit of man
and inhaling the spirit of God.

Edwin Keith

Yielding To His Choreography
Rehearsal Four

What common elements do a storm, a huge fish, a large plant, a stinging wind and the movie, Failure To Launch, have in common? Each one is an object lesson in the havoc we create when we do not follow God's plan.

Matthew McConaughey stars in the 2006 movie about a 35 year old man, who seemingly has it all. He has a great job, an expensive sports car, a sailboat, and a beautiful house. The only trouble is, the house belongs to his parents and they want him to grow up and move out. His parents conspire to "Launch" him into the world.

God writes the choreography for our lives to prepare us to live as Kingdom citizens when we are thrust into the world. Regardless of what happens, or the obstacles we face, He desires we live in a manner worthy of the gospel of Jesus Christ; shining as stars in a dark world. (Philippians 1 & 2)

In Rehearsal Four, we will consider the contrast of yielding to God's choreography for our lives with the destruction produced when we demand our own way. We begin with the example of Jonah, who repeatedly failed to submit to God's plans. Jonah behaved like a rebellious child. He not only defied God, but sulked when he did not get his way.

The Storm
Read Jonah 1:1-16

In this passage, we see Jonah not only resisted God's commands, he actually boarded a ship to go in the opposite direction God told him to go.

Why did Jonah want to go to Tarshish?

Read Genesis 3:1
What phrase did Satan attribute to God in this passage?

What did God actually say to Adam in Genesis?

Do you think Jonah may have justified his actions by asking the question, "Did God really say"?

Comparing our culture to the society in which Jonah lived, do you think defiance of God's will, places us and those in our sphere of influence in greater jeopardy today, than rebellion in Jonah's day?

The Huge Fish
Read: Jonah 1:17 – 3:3

What happened to Jonah?

What did he do?

How did God respond?

Where did Jonah go?

The Plant, The Worm & The Wind
Read: Jonah 4:1-11

How did Jonah respond to God's change of plans to destroy Nineveh?

How did God demonstrate His mercy to Jonah in verse 6?

Proverbs 11:2 contrast pride with humility. According to this passage, what is the result of pride?

The shelter Jonah chose in the plant was transient. God invited Jonah to run from that temporary refuge into the everlasting shelter of His embrace.

Read Romans 8:31-39

What can separate us from the love of God?

<u>Yielding To His Purpose</u>

There is a perception that yielding is a passive act. A word study reveals the opposite. Scripture records many instances where persons model obedience and history is changed. Yielding to God's plan requires courage and trust.

Read the following Scripture references. Identify the person and describe how they responded in obedience to God.

Genesis 12:1-4

Genesis 6:9-22

Luke 1:30 – 38

Matthew 4:18-20

Luke 23:46

Jonah 3:1-3

Personal Reflection

These examples and many more in scripture give witness to the incredible mercy of God's grace. When we yield to His choreography, we have the assurance He will be with us even when we encounter difficulties.

Personal Response

Trusting the shelter of God's embrace. Psalm 91:1

Imagine you are at the circus. It is time for the High Wire Trapeze Performance. The performers are in place. Tension builds. The "catcher" stands alert, waiting. Her only responsibility is to stretch out her hands and trust the "flyer" will be there to pull her back up.

The "flyer" assumes position, calculating when to soar. In the breathtaking choreography of this moment, the "flyer" releases, swooping to a breath stopping dive before swinging back up to join the "catcher" and pull her to safety.

Before the performers can be caught, they must let go. Before they let go, they must trust.

Yielding to the Master's choreography frees us to live with active expectation as we trust He is always there; both to catch us and to give us wings to fly as we dance with Him.

In this exercise are you the flyer, the catcher or a spectator?

Which position would you like to perfect?

More importantly, which role is God inviting you perform?

Grow flowers of gratitude in the soil of prayer

Terri Guillemets

Gratitude answers grace like an echo in a canyon

Ben Patterson

EMBRACE HIS GOODNESS

Rehearsal Five

Goodness is synonymous with God. The church I attended some years ago reinforced this truth every Sunday. At the beginning of the service, the music director would say, "God is good". The congregation responded, "All The Time." The music director would affirm, "All the time". You already know the refrain, "God is good."

For many, Psalm 23 is a favorite Psalm. This Psalm concludes with these words, "Surely goodness and mercy will follow me all the days of my life and I will dwell in the house of the Lord forever." His goodness both precedes and follows us. Where God is, goodness dwells. In this Rehearsal, we will witness God's goodness in many diverse circumstances.

Two synonyms for goodness are kindness and compassion. In the following passages which of the descriptive terms; goodness, kindness, or compassion is used to define God's grace? You may also wish to list other words from these verses which describe God's goodness.

Psalm 34:8

Psalm 103:13

Ephesians 2:7

James 5:11

Romans 11:22

Matthew 9:36

Nehemiah 9:19

Lamentations 3:21-23

> In what practical ways might we experience hope by being attentive to God's goodness in everyday circumstances?

Personal Reflection

Read Genesis 50:20 and Romans 8:28. Joseph suffered unspeakable hardship as the result of his brothers' betrayal. Because Joseph had experienced the great goodness of God, he was able to extend grace to his brothers. In the face of repeated betrayal by persons Joseph trusted, he modeled grace because his confidence was in God. How do these two passages provide hope when we are facing challenging times? Recall a time in your life when you experienced God's goodness during a time of difficulty or grief.

Personal Response

The great goodness of God's grace is evident in every sunrise and sunset. Indeed, in every breath we take. When we welcome Him into the details of our lives, He saturates us with His love. Talk with him about your joys and your problems, just as you would a friend. Goodness, kindness, and compassion will begin to permeate your relationships. Almost imperceptibly, His fragrance will infuse your world.

Write your own version of Psalms 23. Three examples are provided. Use one of these as a guide or use any format you desire.

Psalm 23 *(Today's English Version)*
The Lord is my Shepherd:
I have everything I need.
He lets me rest in fields of green grass
And leads me to quiet pools of fresh water.
He gives me new strength.
He guides me in the right paths,as He promised.
Even though I go through the deepest darkness,
I will not be afraid, Lord,
For You are with me.
Your shepherd's rod and staff protect me.
You prepare a banquet for me…
You welcome me as an honored guest
And fill my cup to the brim.
I know that your goodness and love
Will be with me all my life;
And Your house will be my home
As long as I live.

A Personal Prayer Psalm - Good Shepherd

Psalm 23

Thank you for being my Shepherd.
You have proved yourself faithful in my life.

You are my Shepherd.
I have everything I need.
You are my peace.
You allow me to rest beside the quiet pools of your grace.
You give me strength for each day.
You have guided me in paths of righteousness.

You are my Shepherd.
Even when I face the deepest darkness,
My confidence is always in You.
Your Shepherd's rod and staff protect me.
Your mercies are new every morning.
Your faithfulness is absolute.

You provide everything I need.
My life is enriched through the love of Godly friends.
They are your angels of mercy, O Lord.

When I enter into your presence in prayer,
You welcome me as an honored guest.
Empower me to be your faithful servant.
Because you are my Shepherd,
I know your goodness and love will be with me all my
life.

Thank you, Good Shepherd, for the assurance
Your house will be my home for all eternity.

Amen

My Personal Twenty Third Psalm
The Lord Is My King

The Lord is my King; as His subject,
I shall not lack access to His throne.
He makes me heir to the riches of His Kingdom.
He clothes me in the righteousness of His Son.
He refreshes me through the wind of His Spirit.
He provides level paths for my feet to follow
For the praise of His glory.

Though I walk in a world of confusion, corruption
and chaos, I will fear no evil;
For I am protected by His hand.

Your priestly intercession and your royal discipline
delight me.
You open the way for me in the presence of ridicule
and opposition.
You anoint my head with the holy oil of your Spirit;
My life overflows with your goodness.

Surely, abundant grace and the riches of your
mercy will both precede and follow me all the days
of my life,

And I will dwell in the presence of The King Most
High forever.

Except for the point, the still point, there would be no dance, and there is only the dance.

T.S. Eliot

Rest In His Embrace

Rehearsal Six

Moments spent in the embrace of the Father are moments of serenity for the soul. We encounter God not only in buildings crafted of wood and steel and glass, but we sense His restorative presence as we are mindful of His touch in the crush of our days. This healing interlude occurs as we become responsive to the invitation Jesus extends in the gospel of Matthew.

Matthew 11:28-30   The Message
Are you tired? Worn out? Burned out on religion? Come to me. Get away with me and you'll recover your life. I'll show you how to take a real rest. Walk with me and work with me. Watch how I do it. Learn the unforced rhythms of grace. I won't lay anything heavy or ill-fitting on you. Keep company with me and you'll learn to live freely and lightly."

> In the above passage, identify three postures Jesus refers to which implies the relationship He invites us to enjoy as both active and passive. In other words, it encompasses both attitude and action.

Read Mark 6:30-32

> Imagine the excitement of the disciples as they described for Jesus their ministry tour. (Mark 6:7-12). In your own words, describe Jesus' leadership and compassion for them in verse 31.

Read Genesis 2:2-3

In this passage, who rested?

Have you considered rest as a holy act of worship?

The Embrace of The Father

In Luke 15, Jesus relates the story of the lost sheep, the lost coin, and the lost son. Collectively, they are known as "The Lost Parables". Shortly before Rembrandt died, he painted his masterpiece; Return of The Prodigal Son. A reproduction of that painting, viewed in an office in France, became the inspiration for one of Henri Nouwen's most beloved books, The Return of The Prodigal Son. No where else in scripture is the tenderness of God the Father described more beautifully than in Luke 15: 11-31.

Read Luke 15:11 - 31

This parable is an astounding illustration of God's love for his children. List the words from verse 20 used to describe the father.

In Rembrandt's painting, the Father blesses his son through his tender embrace. Nouwen says this is where sin and forgiveness intersect. " A Father who from the beginning of creation, has stretched out his arms in merciful blessing, not forcing himself

66

on anyone, but always waiting, never letting his arms drop down in despair, but always hoping that his children will return so he can speak words of love to them and let his arms rest on their shoulders."

> Based on the actions of the father in this parable, how might we expect God to respond when we stop running and step into His embrace?

> Do you envision this as a place of quiet rest or one of recrimination? Why?

Personal Reflection

Imagine you are the prodigal son. What thoughts do you have as you experience your Father's embrace? In this parable, the father offers consolation and comfort not condemnation. There is joy and welcome when his rebellious son returns home.

In what way does this narrative help you comprehend that you are fully accepted, loved and embraced by God?

Personal Response

From the words and phrases you identified from Luke 15:11 - 31, write a brief description of God as He is revealed in these verses.

Now, quiet your thoughts and allow yourself to rest in the Father's embrace. Experience the fatigue melting away in the refreshing welcome of His love.

Let them praise His name in the dance.

Psalm 149:3

It is not the answers that show us the way,
it is the questions.

R.M. Rilke

Desiring God
Rehearsal Seven

Prayer is response to intimacy with God. Has your relationship with Christ changed as you began to view prayer as an intimate relationship to be cultivated?

PRAYER DANCE

Pleasure of His Company

Reflection / Confession

Abiding in Him

Yielding to His choreography

Embrace His goodness

Rest in His embrace

Desiring God

Accept His Invitation

Notice His presence

Connect with others

Express His love through my life

Prayer as Dance, is not a formula, or a gimmick. It is simply a tool to help us delve deeper into a more meaningful relationship with Christ. When we comprehend how much God loves us, the pursuit is reciprocal. We find ourselves desiring to spend time with Him. Desiring God is not just an intellectual exercise, it is an emotional encounter.

Our desire to know Him intimately, involves our intellect, our will and our emotions. Jesus declared the greatest commandment is to love God with all our heart, soul and mind. Matthew 22:37

When we encounter the God of scripture who says, "I Am that I Am", our immediate response is worship. Thanksgiving is appreciation for what God has done. Praise acknowledges who He is. Our praise becomes adoration. Adoration is not the same as praise but praise results in adoration.

I love you, O Lord, my strength. The Lord is my rock, my fortress, and my deliverer; my God is my rock, in whom I take refuge. He is my shield and the Horn of my salvation, my stronghold. I call to the Lord who is worthy of praise. Psalm 18:1-3a

Who is the object of our worship?

Circle meaningful words from Psalm 18:1-3a that describe characteristics of God.

How are we invited to express praise to God from: Psalm 149:3 and Psalm 150?

List the characteristics of God you find in the following verses:

1 John 4:8

Romans 15:33

Romans 15:5

II Corinthians 12:9

Romans 15:33

II Corinthians 1:3

What does Luke 1:45 - 47 reveal to us about Mary, the mother of Jesus?

Where did her praise begin?

Whom was she praising?

What portion of your prayers are focused on worship and praise?

Personal Reflection
The following meditation is designed to focus our attention toward being cognizant of simply adoring God and desiring to spend time with Him.

Begin by quieting your thoughts. Ask God to help you experience this time not so much as an assignment to complete but an occasion to enjoy the pleasure of His company.

Read Psalms 95 - 100 (out loud if possible) Read through the passage a second time.

You might consider reading one chapter each day, or use this as a time of extended prayer and meditation during the week.

Personal Response
When we encounter the living Christ, our response is worship. The outflow of adoration is praise, thanksgiving, confession, and surrender.

When we step into the embrace of the Bridegroom, the symphony of His love cascades around us.

As we become aware of His presence, the temptation is to think ourselves beyond the reach of His grace. And yet, it is the gracious mercy of His love that envelopes us and invites us to come to Him. He bids us, "Come all of you who are weak and weary and I will give you rest."

He invites you to dance with Him because He takes great delight in you. Zephaniah 3:17

Pray a prayer or write a letter in your journal expressing your desire to love Jesus and honor Him with your life.

Prayer is when you talk to God;
meditation is when you listen to Him.

Author Unknown

Accept His Invitation
Rehearsal Eight

YOU ARE CORDIALLY INVITED

To Attend
A Wedding Banquet

In Honor of
Jesus, the Bridegroom

This banquet will be held
at the Father's house.
The Father is well connected.
Many notable celebrities will be in attendance.
Some of the persons who have reserved include:
Moses, Abe & Sarah, Joseph and his family,
Ruth & Boaz, Noah and his clan,
Mary Magdalene,
eleven of the disciples,
Paul, and John the Beloved.
(Protocol requires you do not divulge your surprise or
disdain when members of the family appear, whom
you do not expect.)

Please invite your family and friends
Everyone is invited, however each person must
personally accept the invitation.
The Father's resources are unlimited.
He has spared no expense
in planning this lavish event.
The celebration begins when you
accept this invitation.
Directions: John 3:16 or Jeremiah 33:3

The time of the inaugural ceremony
has yet to be determined.
This is one of the mysteries
that will keep the evening interesting.

Chariots will be at our disposal
to transport guests to an undisclosed
location, identified as heaven.

The Father invites you to come as you are.
Don't be concerned
if your clothes are dirty or torn.
His counterpart, the Holy Spirit,
has prepared new clothing for you.
Please save the date, because all of the
family will be magnificent
in their royal robes.

Father said your ticket has been paid in full.
It is free but the cost was not cheap. Jesus, the
Bridegroom, spent some agonizing hours to procure
your admission.

Please R.S.V.P to the Palace
as soon as possible.

Father will take care of all the details.
He will explain everything you need to know
from His Book. Father is patient, but you need
to RSVP to the palace as soon as possible.
You will not have the option
of observing from the gate.

Matthew 22:1-12 is a fascinating parable that tells the story of a King who planned a wedding feast for his son, but the people he invited would not come. The feast was ready. What was he to do? He sent his servants out into the streets to bring everyone who would come to the party. Guess who came to dinner.

Read Matthew 22:1-13

How do you define the word, parable?

Identify the main characters in this parable:

The King: _____

The Son: _____

The people who were pre-invited (see Deuteronomy 29:9-13)

The servants: _____

The crowds: _____

The man not properly attired: _____

Why did the King plan a banquet for his son?

What excuses did the invited guests use to avoid the invitation?

What does verse 6 tell us about the level of opposition to the king?

The people who were pre-invited to the wedding feast, killed the kings' servants.

Who did the king instruct his new servants to bring to the banquet?

Can you describe what you believe to be the wedding clothes the host made reference to in verses 10 & 11?

Why do you think the king invited the man and then had him thrown out?

Present Day Feast

How would you describe this story in spiritual terms? In other words, what lesson does Jesus want to teach from this parable?

How do you think this story parallels our culture today?

Read Revelation 19:4-9

In this passage, who is the Lamb?

Who is the bride?

The bride wore fine linen. What does "fine linen" represent?

Personal Reflection
Have you received your invitation to the marriage of the Lamb? Have you opened it or is it tossed aside with your junk mail? There were three groups of people represented in this parable; the ones who celebrated, the indifferent and the hostile. Which group would you hang with? God's Secret Service will be vetting persons who attempt to enter the Marriage of the Lamb.

Do you have proper ID? Are you clothed appropriately? Have you traded your rags of self-righteousness for the riches of His holiness?

Personal Response
Read Ephesians 6:10-18. Make a list of the clothing you will receive. The Father said it is important to wear these garments at all times so you have protection from malicious attack.

As you discard your filthy rags in preparation to attend this banquet, the King's Son will replace them with robes of righteousness. Your new wardrobe has been purchased by the Bridegroom Himself. These garments have been requisitioned especially for you. The Father only asks that you wear them with honor. In Kingdom Clothes, you are a reflection of His glory.

Final Preparations

You have been invited to the greatest celebration of all time. My prayer is that you will call John 3:16 to RSVP today. It is advised that you use the buddy system and make the call with a trusted Kingdom Official. Prayer lines are open 24/7. Please call now.

We must move from asking God to take care of the
things that are breaking our hearts, to praying
about the things that are breaking his heart.

Margaret Gibb

Notice His Presence

Rehearsal Nine

Have you taken notice of God's presence today? Are you mindful of the sacred in seemingly ordinary events?

Noticing the presence of God is as simple as listening, but as profound as hearing. It is as simple as opening our eyes, but as profound as seeing. It is as simple as reaching out to touch a neighbor, and as profound as feeling the texture of the hem of Jesus garment.

Experiencing the presence of God is available to everyone. It is sought by many but recognized by few. God never ceases to reveal Himself. The question is, are we too busy to notice?

Day after day the heavens pour forth speech. The heavens declare the glory of God.
Psalm 19:1-6

In the crush of our days, sometimes we wonder if God takes notice of us. Does He choreograph my days? In Scripture we read the story of an anxious mother-in-law who almost turned the waltz of romance into a tango laced with regret. The kinsman-redeemer would not be seduced. Through the integrity of following God's timing, he increased his estate and won the heart of his beautiful bride.

The love story of Ruth and Boaz provides compelling insight into God's provision for a nation who experienced a famine. Those circumstances were part of His plan to maintain the blood line of His Son, Jesus.

During this Rehearsal, we will revisit two incidents where God reveals His presence. We will observe to what extent He takes notice of His people. We will be invited to follow His lead. We will practice being attentive to the choreography of His grace.

God Takes Notice of His People
Based on The Book of Ruth
The Holy Bible

It has been an exhilarating day. I just gave birth to a son. His name is Obed. But wait, let me tell you the story from the beginning……..

My name is Ruth. I am from the country of Moab. More than ten years ago, Bethlehem of Judea was experiencing a terrible famine. Because there was no food; Naomi, her husband and two sons moved to the country where I lived. I married one of Naomi's sons. After some years, my father-in-law, brother-in-law and husband died. Only the women are left now. We must see to everything. How long must I endure this unending fatigue and loneliness?

It took some time, but eventually we adjusted to our loss. At least I had my own people and my sister-in-law, Orpah to talk with. Naomi means well but she can sometimes be very harsh in her bitterness.

When the famine was over, Naomi decided to go back to Bethlehem, to her people. But Orpah and I have roots here. My people are here. Naomi must have sensed our hesitation because as we walked to Judea, she gave Orpah and me permission to return to Moab. Orpah went back, but I decided to stay with Naomi. It did not seem good for her to return alone. I told Naomi I would go with her. Where she goes I will go and where she stays I will stay. Her people will be my people and her God will be my God. Naomi is the mother of the man I loved. She is my only link to his family and to his God.

As we arrived in Bethlehem, the barley harvest had just begun. I gleaned in the fields beginning at sunrise. It was pretty scary out there. I battled heat, thirst and hunger. At times I was afraid I would have to battle the harvesters as well. Rumors of abuse and violence circulated like wildfire.

One morning, while we were gleaning in the field, I looked up. Perhaps it was the heat and the need of the harvesters for a diversion. There was a current of excitement spreading across the fields. Boaz, the owner of the fields had arrived. The people seem to like him. The harvesters greet him warmly and with respect. As it happens, he is a trustworthy person. He gave me permission to glean in his fields. Not only that, he encouraged me with kind words of blessing.

According to Naomi, Boaz is our kinsman-redeemer. Naomi told me to remind Boaz he is our nearest relative and to spend the night with him on the threshing floor. I did everything Naomi told me to do. When Boaz awoke, and found me lying at his feet, he asked who I was. He was a perfect gentleman. He told me there was actually a relative, closer than he, who is my kinsman-redeemer.

Boaz was very wise. He called ten elders together as his witnesses and invited the other relative to buy my father-in-law Elimelech's land and claim me as his wife. Because he refused; Boaz was permitted to purchase all the family property from Naomi and I became his bride.

This is actually where my story began. The blessing of the elders was realized today as God blessed us with a son, Obed. Only later would I realize how the favor of God rested on me today. Obed became the father of Jesse, who was the father of David. Who would have thought me, a Moabite woman would be among the blood line of my true Kinsman-Redeemer, Jesus?

It is sometimes difficult to understand how God works everything, even the difficult things, for our good and for His eternal glory.

My heart resounds with the same joy Mary expressed generations later as she prepared for Jesus' birth,

"My soul glorifies the Lord and my spirit rejoices in God my Savior, for He is mindful of the humble state of His servant."

I am blessed among women, because my Lord has noticed me and heard my cry. Our God is ever mindful of His people.

What did Ruth stand to lose in order to remain loyal to Naomi? (Ruth 2:11)

Contrast the consequences of Ruth and Orpah's decision. (Ruth 1:15,16)

From Ruth: Chapter 2, list various ways God showed His favor to Ruth.

v.8 _____

v.9 _____

v.12 _____

v.14 _____

v.15 _____

v.16 _____

Referencing Matthew 1:1-16 with Ruth 4:11-12, how was the blessing of the elders in Ruth 4:11 fulfilled?

From whom did Ruth draw courage and strength to remain faithful in the midst of adversity? Ruth 2:11-12

Being Mindful of God's Presence
The Road To Emmaus Luke 24:13-35

Read Luke 24:13-16

Who was traveling to Emmaus and where had they been?

Who joined them as they walked?

Do we have an inclination to expect Jesus and acknowledge His presence as we participate in the routine events of our day?

Read Luke 24:17-24

What events were the two persons discussing when Jesus joined them?

In your own words, describe what Cleopas told Jesus about the events they witnessed.

Why do you think the two believers did not recognize Jesus?

Read Luke 24:25-29

What role did Jesus assume with them as they walked to Emmaus?

Read Luke 24:30-35

When did they recognize Jesus?

What was their response?

In your experience, are you sometimes ambivalent or hesitant about acknowledging Jesus' presence?

Personal Reflection
When has Jesus met you on your journey at a time you least expected Him?

Personal Response
Spend a few quiet moments thinking about Jesus. What practical steps could you take to become more aware of His presence in your day to day activities? As you meditate on the two who walked with Jesus to Emmaus and the story of Ruth, you might choose to write in your journal, draw a picture, sing a song or take a reflective nature walk to express your gratitude that Jesus takes notice of your life and has a plan for you. Ask God to help you be mindful of Him.

Remember, "When we cannot see His hand, we can always trust His heart".

When we become present to God and to
His people, our step becomes lighter because
God has called others out to dance also.

Henri Nouwen

Connect With Others
Rehearsal Ten

Paul's Practice of Passionate Persuasion

The Apostle Paul was the consummate Biblical example of someone who knew how to build a network of support and interface with others. His passion for the Gospel was expressed through his concern for people. Before his transformational meeting with the Lord on the Damascus road he was known as Saul. Saul was his Hebrew name. His Greek name, Paul was used after he began his ministry to the Gentiles. His gregarious personality was evident even then. Billy Graham is a modern day example of a charismatic person who is sold out to God. Prayer is significant in the ministry of both men.

It was imperative for Paul to become a follower of Christ before he could connect with people and introduce them to Christ. In a sense, Paul was the link, as a ring in a chain that provided the connection that shaped the history of Christianity.

Through Paul's letters to the early churches, he revealed his methodology of interfacing with believers. God invites us to cultivate a connective ministry of goodwill. The nexus of curiosity established when we are ambassadors for Christ, becomes the precursor to persons moving from seekers to followers. This Rehearsal will reveal the pattern Paul crafted as he spread the gospel to the Gentiles.

The Incredible Web of God's Grace

Read Acts 22:1-14

What were Paul's credentials?

By his own admission, how did he use his influence and privilege?

When did Paul's priorities change?

Read Philippians 1:1-11

What was Paul's attitude toward the people of Philippi?

List the essence of Paul's intercession for them.

Have you used this prayer as a model to pray for someone? Write a brief account of that experience.

Did Paul minister as a lone ranger? Who was with him? What is the significance of Paul having supportive associates with him?

What gift did Paul pray God would grant the Philippians at the close of this letter? (Phil. 4:23)

Read Ephesians 1:15-19

List the things Paul prayed for the Ephesians in this passage.

Read Ephesians 3:14-20 and Ephesians 6:21-24

Paul identifies his helper, Tychicus,

as: _____

and _____

Who comprises the family of God?

What is the theme of Paul's prayer?

How does verse 20 empower us to persevere in prayer even when we do not perceive our prayers are being answered?

At the close of this letter, (Eph. 6:24) what gift did Paul pray for God to grant the Ephesians?

Read Colossians 1:1-8 & 4:7

> List four of the nine persons Paul identifies who minister with him in Rome.

Read Colossians 1:9-14

> From verse 9 & 10, what was the two pronged dimension of Paul's prayer for the believers of Colosse? List five things Paul prayed for them.

NOTE: Paul was reminding them in their own vernacular, "Spiritual impression without spiritual expression, leads to spiritual depression.

Read Colossians 4:18

> At the close of this letter, what gift did Paul pray for God to grant the Colossians?

> How do you define grace?

> Grace, Peace and Love are hallmarks of Paul's prayers for the early church. We would do well to use his prayers as a model for intercession.

When God Asks You To Dance, SAY YES!

From Paul's personal letters, the practicality of his practice of persuasion emerges. He weaves a consistent pattern of five principles in his letters to the early churches which are repeated countless times in the thirteen books of the New Testament which he authored.

Five aspects of Paul's dance of ministry included: Preparation, Prayer, Partners, Perseverance, and Persuasion.

Preparation
Paul had not personally met all of the persons to whom he wrote. But, he made it his business to know about them. He addressed them with respect and openness. He was vividly honest about who he was, about his background and about his mission; to bring the Good News of Jesus Christ.

Prayer
The Epistles, as well as all as all of Paul's writings reveal emphatically the importance he placed on prayer. In the first twelve verses of Colossians, Paul makes reference to prayer seven times.

Partner
We all need friends. Godly friends who pray for us, encourage us, and hold us accountable. As accomplished as Paul was, he could not minister effectively alone. Colossians 4:11-18, Paul mentions the people who assisted him while he was in Rome.

Moses told God, I cannot take care of all these people alone, it is too much for me. (Numbers 11:14) We read in Ecclesiastes 4:9, "Two are better than one and a cord of three strands is not easily broken." Jesus called twelve disciples to assist him. The pattern of partnering with others and establishing accountability is documented throughout scripture.

Perseverance

No pain no gain was Paul's motto.

I Corinthians 9:24-27 dispels the accepted wisdom that the Christian life is an easy one. However, Paul encourages us with this promise: if we have a purpose, a plan, preparation and perseverance the prize will be ours. The prize he refers to is a crown that will last for eternity. And, as someone has wisely said, "Eternity begins now."

Persuasion

Paul pleaded, cajoled, worked, wept and prayed for the early Christians. The power of his persuasion was grounded in his authentic love for Christ. With authority, he could command, "Whatever happens, conduct yourselves in a manner worthy of the Gospel."

Personal Reflection

As you identified the pattern of Paul's letters, did you recognize that you are called to accept your own story of failure and redemption? Have you acknowledged you are a precious person filled with grace, called to extend that grace to others? Ours is an account of redemption. It is not a fairy-tale, but a true story of the transforming power of grace. Our story is not yet complete. The ending will be told by our heavenly Father when we step into His embrace for all eternity. The conversion of a life is a miracle of the moment. The completion of a life is the formation of a life span. Philippians 1:6

There is still time to live life abundant, today.

Personal Response

When we choose to live in confident dependence upon the Grace Giver, we experience freedom to step out of our prisons of isolation and into a world that may no longer be part of our comfort zone. Will you express dependence upon Him through a life lived authentically sold out to Christ?

Write your response to the statement, "Whatever happens conduct yourselves in a manner worthy of the gospel." How then shall I live? Philippians 1:27

Prayer is the coin paid to Gratitude.

Jessi Lane Adams

Express His Love
Through My Life
Rehearsal Eleven

We join this Rehearsal in Capernaum, shadow dancing beside Jesus while He ministers in his own home town.

Expressing God's love through our lives is complex in theory, but simple in practice. When we study the life of Jesus, it is evident He lived moment by moment in harmony with His Father. Our inclination is to follow the Pharisaical approach, perceiving that expressing God's love involves complex rules we must adhere to.

Jesus said, "My yoke is easy and my burden is light". It is we who create complexity.

In this Rehearsal, we will glean insight into the question, "How then shall we live?" Through observing Jesus, we will notice four habits Jesus practiced:

- He was observant of those around Him
- He invited persons to be part of His life
- He welcomed   interruptions as opportunities
- Prayer was the language of love He used to communicate with His Father

Read Philippians 1:27

> The principle for expressing God's love through our lives is found in this verse. In

your opinion, how do we "conduct ourselves in a manner worthy of the gospel"?

Jesus Models Four Habits that Expressed God's Love

Habit One: Jesus was observant of the underlying needs in people's lives.

Read Matthew 9:1-8

How did the man's friends help him?

What did Jesus observe that caused him to heal the paralytic?

How did Jesus respond to the criticism of the religious teachers?

What was the result of Jesus' actions? (verses 6- 8)

Habit Two: Jesus invited persons to be part of His life.

Read Matthew 9:9-13

What criticism was directed at Jesus by the Pharisees?

How does Jesus' response bring hope to all people?

Habit Three: Jesus viewed interruptions as opportunity.

Read Matthew 9:18-26

How did the ruler show honor to Jesus?

How was the woman's faith expressed?

How did Jesus reward her faith?

What was the response of the crowd to Jesus' statement the girl was sleeping?

How did Jesus respond to their disdain?

Have you experienced ridicule because of your faith? If so, how has this event impacted you?

Habit Four: Prayer. Jesus stayed in constant communion with His Father.

"Lord, teach us to pray." The only occasion recorded in Scripture in which the disciples asked Jesus to teach them a skill, is recorded in Luke 11:1. One of the disciples asked Jesus to teach them to pray. This speaks volumes about His prayer life.

As you read the following Scriptures what do you observe about the prayer life of Jesus? When did He Pray? Who was with Him as He prayed?

Matthew 14:23

Matthew 26:26

Matthew 14:19

Mark 1:35

Luke 5:16

Do not be anxious about anything, but in everything, by prayer and petition, with thanksgiving present your requests to God. Philippians 4:6

Scripture answers Scripture. An old adage proclaims: The Old Testament is the New Testament Concealed; the New Testament is the Old Testament revealed.

Two Old Testament passages offer insight into transforming ordinary days into extraordinary lives.

Read Hosea 12:5-6

>At the beginning of verse 6, what prerequisite does Hosea say is necessary to live a life that brings glory to God?

>What principles does Hosea urge believers to live by?

>For Whom are we to wait? Based on the language Hosea used, do you perceive "waiting on God" as active or passive?

Read Micah 6:5-8

>What does the Lord require of His people?

>In practical terms, how do we practice this concept?

>Micah told the people to "remember their journey". What are the benefits of remembering your pilgrimage with God? Do you keep a gratitude journal?

Personal Reflection

Ultimately, the question each of us must answer is "How then shall I live?" Always and only the answer must be, "I will live to bring God glory." God choreographs a symphony of grace orchestrated upon the pages of life. Our lives reflect God's grace as we live in relationship with Him.

You have been given a ministry. A ministry only you are equipped to fulfill. The ministry of being you. There is only one you, with your distinctive personality and talents. Step into God's larger scheme by following the Holy Spirit. Make a choice every day to be available in whatever way God chooses to use you.

Create space for the glory of God to be manifest through your life. Your step will become lighter as you recognize other dancers along the way. Your shoes will fit perfectly when you follow the steps of Jesus' choreography.

Personal Response

The Invitation:

Jesus invites you to dance. The dance of acceptance. The dance of confession. The dance of yielding. The dance of rest. The dance of His love. He is waiting.

May our world be deluged with people who say, "Yes!" when Jesus extends the invitation; "Will you dance with Me?

Prayer as Dance

All scripture passages are from the NIV unless otherwise noted. Use your favorite translation.

About the Author

Patti A. Gell is an inspirational speaker, retreat leader and author. She lives in Holland, MI and considers Tucson AZ her second home.

Her life verse is Jeremiah 18:3-4. I went down to the Potter's house, and I saw him working at the wheel. But the pot he was shaping from the clay was marred in His hands; so the Potter formed it into another pot, shaping it as seemed best to him.

"Each day God extends an invitation to observe His thumbprint upon my life. The design is uniquely His. When I place myself with reckless abandon upon the Potter's wheel, He reshapes the broken pieces of clay of my life and sculpts them into an exquisite vessel to be filled and poured out for the praise of His glory."

The purpose of this book is to spark attentiveness to the indelible touch of grace upon each life. Let's see if the Potter is in now, shall we?

Choreography of Grace Worship Seminars

Our Mission

The Mission of GracePage Ministries is to spark awareness to the invitation to enjoy a dynamic relationship with God through the practice of prayer.
Jeremiah 18:1-6

CHOREOGRAPHY OF GRACE RETREATS UTILIZE

God's Inerrant Word • Break Out Sessions
Praise & Prayer • Interactive Group Activities
Teaching • Solo Reflection • and more...

Your invitation is found in Psalm 150:4

Participants will be invited to experience deeper intimacy with Christ and unity with one another. The heart of God is love. He invites us to know Him and be known by Him.

Contact and Booking:
GracePage Ministries
Patti A. Gell
gracepageministries@gmail.com
www.gracepage.org

GracePage Ministries

unprepared for the onslaught of mercy unleashed through a mother's ceaseless prayer and devoted care.

The definitive meaning of my middle name; Ann is grace. Inscribed on page after page of my life is the symphony of God's grace. Sometimes, grace came when I least expected it. Sometimes, only after I had run hard in pursuit of it. I have experienced grace as bright as a blinding neon light in a dark alley and as subtle as the rays of the morning sunrise on a murky day.

Frankly, I have a hard time trying to pigeonhole grace. God's grace is at once amazing, tenacious, marvelous and mystifying. Grace is both an adjective descriptive of God's character and an adverb denoting His power. Grace lavishes the essence of His presence into our world.

There is much I have yet to learn about grace. But this much I know for sure. Grace has been my constant companion on this pilgrimage of life. Grace invited me to take the first tenuous step of faith and grace will journey with me as I dance the first waltz with my King.

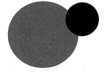

Patti A Gell